I0824876

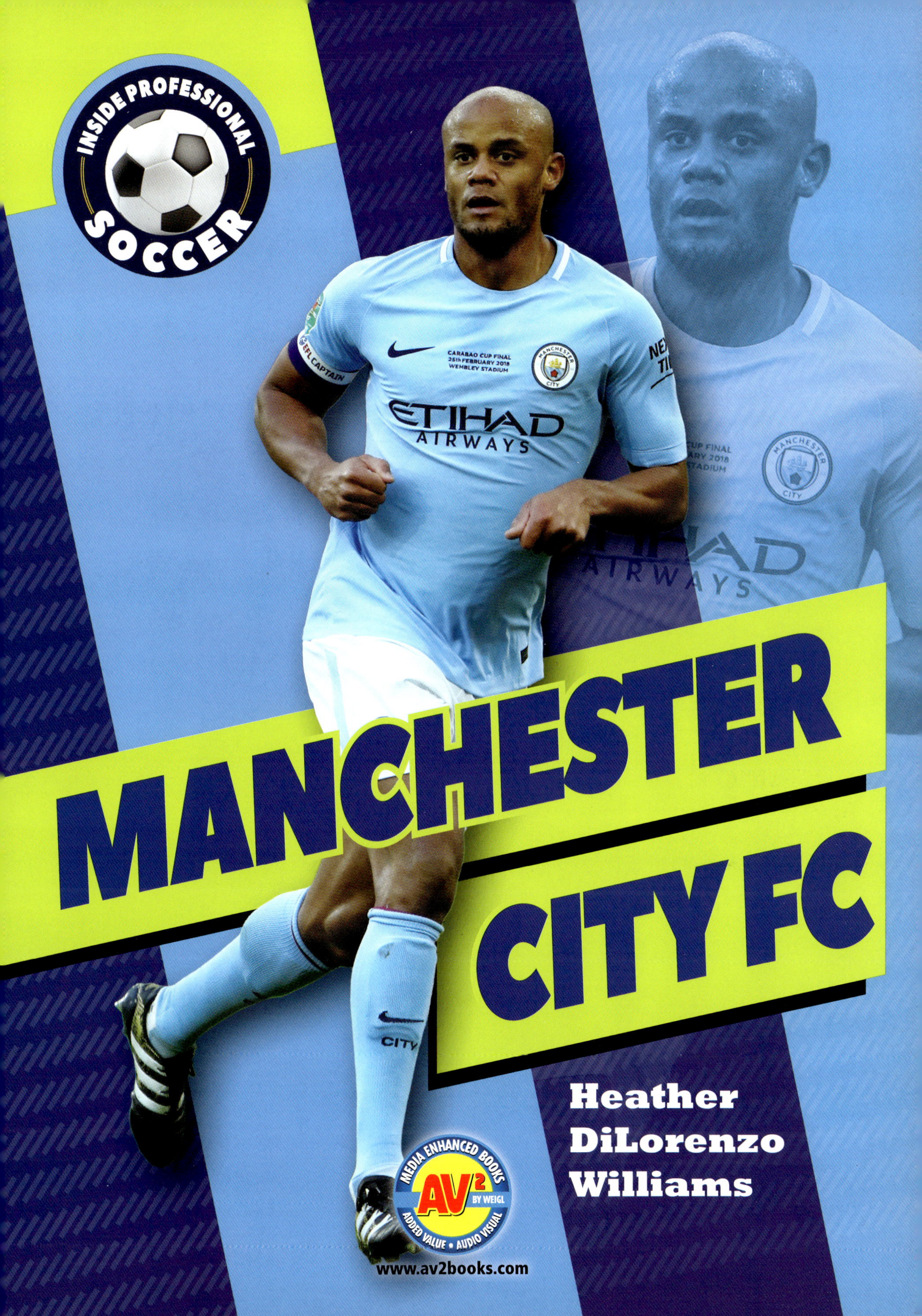
INSIDE PROFESSIONAL
SOCCER
MANCHESTER
CITY FC
Heather
DiLorenzo
Williams
MEDIA ENHANCED BOOKS
AV2
BY WEIGL
ADDED VALUE • AUDIO VISUAL
www.av2books.com

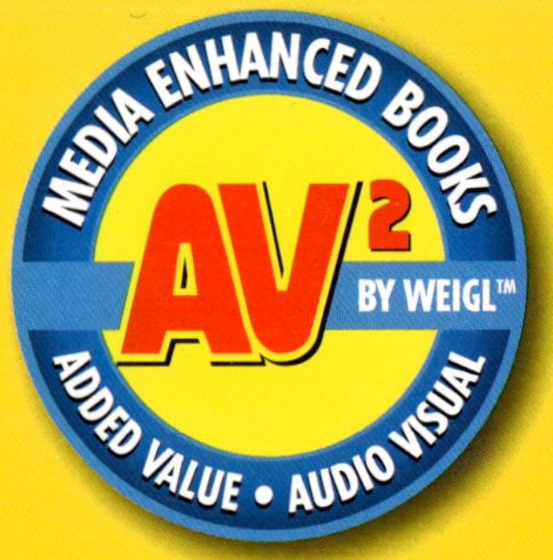

Go to www.av2books.com, and enter this book's unique code.

BOOK CODE

AVU44277

AV² by Weigl brings you media enhanced books that support active learning.

AV² provides enriched content that supplements and complements this book. Weigl's AV² books strive to create inspired learning and engage young minds in a total learning experience.

Your AV² Media Enhanced books come alive with...

Audio
Listen to sections of the book read aloud.

Key Words
Study vocabulary, and complete a matching word activity.

Video
Watch informative video clips.

Quizzes
Test your knowledge.

Embedded Weblinks
Gain additional information for research.

Slide Show
View images and captions, and prepare a presentation.

Try This!
Complete activities and hands-on experiments.

... and much, much more!

Published by AV² by Weigl
350 5th Avenue, 59th Floor
New York, NY 10118
Website: www.av2books.com

Library of Congress Control Number: 2018968482

ISBN 978-1-7911-0607-2 (hardcover)
ISBN 978-1-7911-0608-9 (multi-user eBook)
ISBN 978-1-7911-0609-6 (single-user eBook)

Printed in Guangzhou, China
1 2 3 4 5 6 7 8 9 0 23 22 21 20 19

022019
102318

Project Coordinator: John Willis Designer: Terry Paulhus

Every reasonable effort has been made to trace ownership and to obtain permission to reprint copyright material. The publishers would be pleased to have any errors or omissions brought to their attention so that they may be corrected in subsequent printings.

The publisher acknowledges Alamy, Getty Images, and iStock as its primary image suppliers for this title.

CONTENTS

Introduction

In the late 1880s, two soccer **clubs** were born in the city of Manchester, England. These small clubs would evolve into two of soccer's most famous rivals. One team, Manchester United, skyrocketed to the top of the ranks. The other team has bounced between golden ages of success and dark days of failure throughout its history. That team is Manchester City Football Club (FC).

Unpredictability is one quality that makes Manchester City unique. Manchester City, or simply City, has been known to beat the top team in its league, only to lose to a much lower ranked team a few weeks later. City is one of 20 teams in Great Britain's Premier League. It is the only team in Premier League history to have both won the league championship and been **relegated** to a lower division. Although City has a history of ups and downs, the team is currently in one of its greatest periods of success yet.

David Silva is considered one of the most talented Manchester City players of all time. He averages one goal every two games.

Nicolás Otamendi left Valencia for Manchester City in 2015. He also plays for his home country of Argentina in international competitions, including the World Cup.

MANCHESTER CITY FC

Arena Etihad Stadium

Division English Premier League

Head Coach Pep Guardiola

Location Manchester, England

FIFA Club World Cups 0

Nicknames City, Sky Blues, Citizens

16 Players in the 2018 World Cup

27 Total Trophies

3 Home Stadiums

80 Years at Maine Road Stadium

55,097 Seats at Etihad Stadium

History

Management decided to change the team's name from Gorton Association Football Club and Ardwick to Manchester City in 1894. A fan club today called 1894 Group honors the team's history.

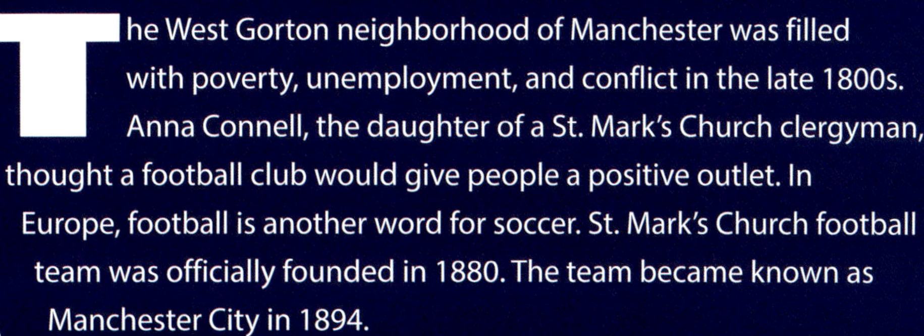

The West Gorton neighborhood of Manchester was filled with poverty, unemployment, and conflict in the late 1800s. Anna Connell, the daughter of a St. Mark's Church clergyman, thought a football club would give people a positive outlet. In Europe, football is another word for soccer. St. Mark's Church football team was officially founded in 1880. The team became known as Manchester City in 1894.

Manchester City won the Football Association (FA) Cup in 1904. For the next 30 years, the team faced money issues and many losses. After big wins in the 1930s, City did not win another trophy until 1956. The team entered another golden age between 1965 and 1976. Manchester City won the league championship, the FA Cup, the League Cup, and the prestigious European Cup Winners' Cup. However, City did not win another title for more than three decades after this period.

The 1990s and 2000s saw more ups and downs, including the club's lowest-ever performance in 1998. That year, Manchester City was dropped to the lowest division of professional soccer. In 2008, the wealthy Abu Dhabi United Group purchased Manchester City. The new owners hired top players and some of soccer's top coaches. Manchester City entered one of its most successful periods to date. City has won the Premier League title three times since 2011.

Shortly after City won the 1904 FA Cup, a series of financial hardships and the loss of their stadium to a fire sent the team into its first of many difficult periods.

The Arena

City Square, a special fan area just outside the stadium, hosts **live entertainment**, **interactive games**, and **special guests** on match days.

Manchester City does not own Etihad Stadium. The club signed a 250-year lease with the City of Manchester in 2002 for the rights to renovate and permanently occupy the stadium.

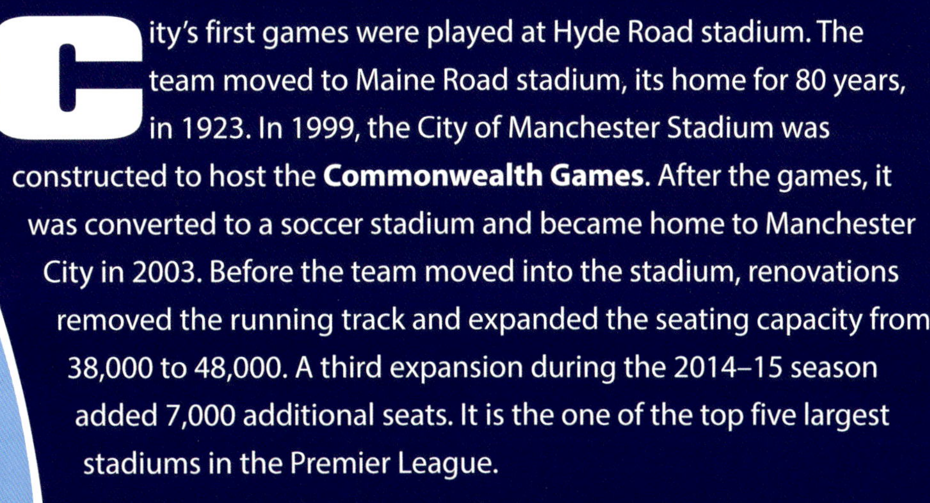

City's first games were played at Hyde Road stadium. The team moved to Maine Road stadium, its home for 80 years, in 1923. In 1999, the City of Manchester Stadium was constructed to host the **Commonwealth Games**. After the games, it was converted to a soccer stadium and became home to Manchester City in 2003. Before the team moved into the stadium, renovations removed the running track and expanded the seating capacity from 38,000 to 48,000. A third expansion during the 2014–15 season added 7,000 additional seats. It is the one of the top five largest stadiums in the Premier League.

The stadium is a rolling oval shape. Its unique transparent roof allows maximum light for the **pitch**, which is a combination of natural and artificial grass. There are four distinct sections of seating, the North Stand, the South Stand, the East Stand, and the Colin Bell Stand. The seats and roof lights are Manchester City's sky blue color.

City of Manchester Stadium was renamed Etihad Stadium in 2011 after one of the team's sponsors. Etihad Stadium has won multiple awards, including a 2004 Inclusive Design Award for accessibility. The stadium provides access for all users, including families with children and fans that use wheelchairs.

After World War II (1939–1945), Maine Road stadium was also home to Manchester City's biggest rival, Manchester United. Most of Manchester United's stadium, Old Trafford, was destroyed by bombs and took eight years to rebuild.

Where They Play

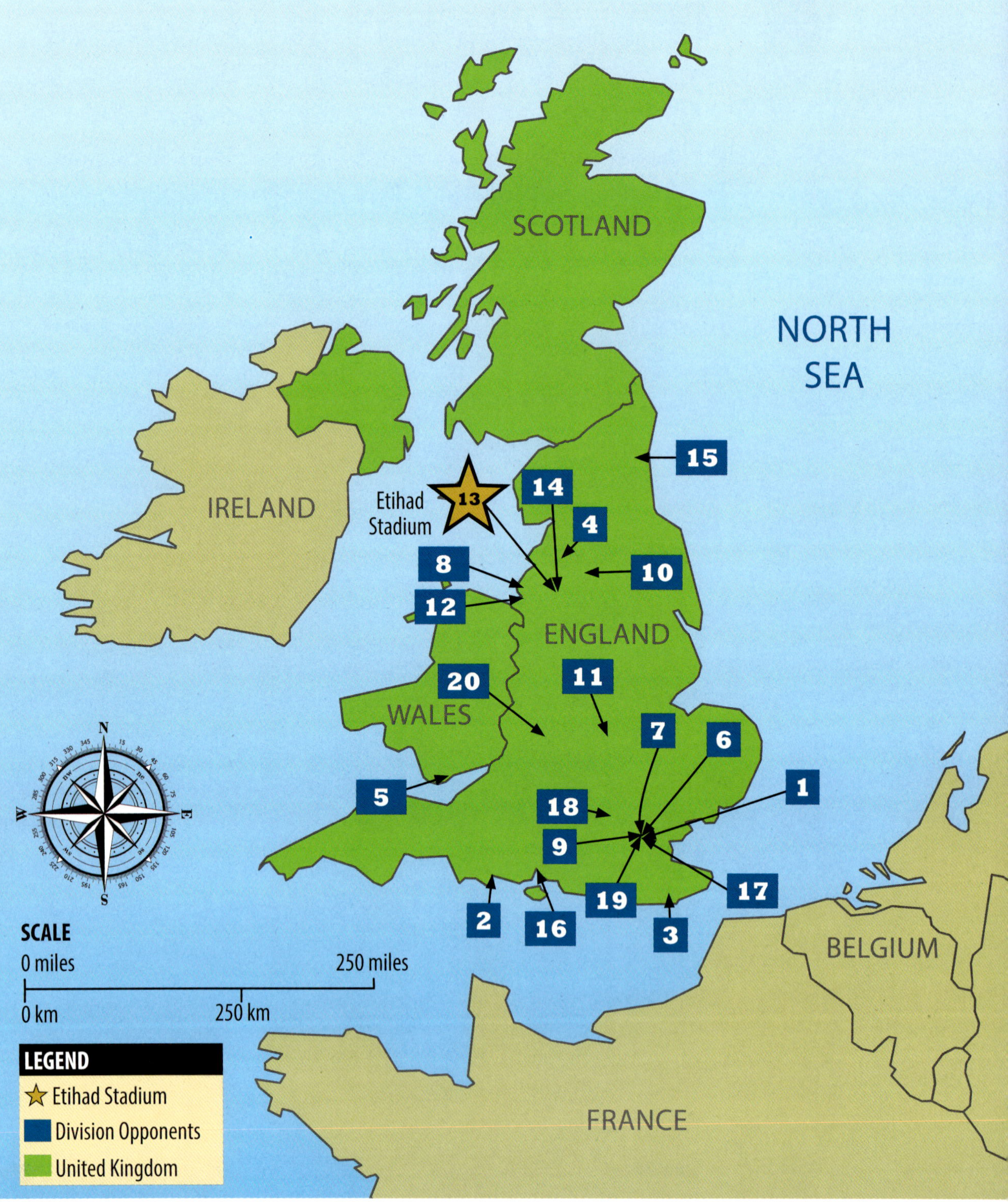

Arena
Etihad Stadium

Location
Manchester, England

Broke Ground
1999

Completed
2002

Field Design
The hybrid pitch, mostly natural grass reinforced by artificial fibers, is more than 20 feet (6 meters) below ground level, creating an ancient Greek amphitheater effect for spectators.

Features
- Twelve steel masts with steel cables support the roof.
- Roof has a curved "roller coaster" appearance.
- Upper tiers are accessed using eight spiral turrets around the stadium.

2018–19 PREMIER LEAGUE TEAMS

1 Arsenal *(Highbury, London, England)*
2 Bournemouth *(Bournemouth, England)*
3 Brighton and Hove Albion *(Brighton and Hove, England)*
4 Burnley *(Burnley, England)*
5 Cardiff City *(Cardiff, Wales)*
6 Chelsea *(West London, England)*
7 Crystal Palace *(South London, England)*
8 Everton *(Liverpool, England)*
9 Fulham *(Hammersmith and Fulham, England)*
10 Huddersfield Town *(Huddersfield, England)*
11 Leicester City *(Leicester, England)*
12 Liverpool *(Liverpool, England)*
★13 Manchester City *(Manchester, England)*
14 Manchester United *(Manchester, England)*
15 Newcastle United *(Newcastle-upon-Tyne, England)*
16 Southampton *(Southampton, England)*
17 Tottenham Hotspur *(North London, England)*
18 Watford *(Watford, England)*
19 West Ham United *(East London, England)*
20 Wolverhampton Wanderers *(Wolverhampton, England)*

The Uniforms

Although Manchester City's home uniform is the same year after year, the club's away uniform changes almost yearly. It often has no connection to the club's colors.

Manchester City's very first uniforms were black jerseys with a white cross on the front. Around 1895, the team's colors became sky blue and white. The current home **kit** consists of a light blue jersey, white shorts, and navy blue socks. City's home uniform has not changed much in more than 100 years.

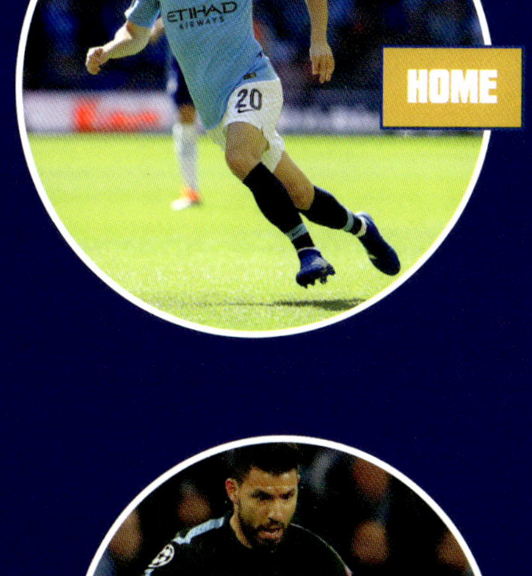

City's away kit has changed over the years. One traditional away kit was red and black, the colors of AC Milan. An assistant coach said wearing the colors of the successful Italian team would inspire City to win. In more recent years, the away uniform has been mostly black with various accent colors.

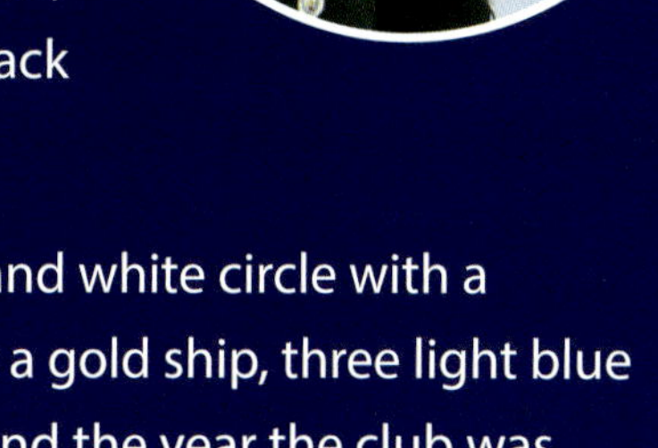

Manchester City's logo is a light blue and white circle with a shield in the center. Inside the shield is a gold ship, three light blue stripes, and a red rose. The club name and the year the club was established are written in blue inside the white circle.

The golden ship on Manchester City's logo represents Manchester's trade history. The diagonal stripes symbolize the three rivers that run through the city.

Goalie Gear

Goalkeepers usually wear bright colors so officials will not mistake them for field players during a match. Ederson Moraes has donned the bright kits of City since the 2017–18 season.

Goalkeepers must stand out from players and officials on the field. Goalies usually wear long sleeves and brightly colored jerseys. Some wear pants instead of shorts. Most goalies wear special goalkeeping gloves. These gloves have rubbery surfaces to help them grip the ball. The gloves sometimes contain plastic spines to protect goalkeepers' hands from injuries.

Manchester City's starting goalkeeper is Ederson Moraes. He is known simply as Ederson. As a child, he had a powerful shot but did not dribble well. Ederson's coach put him in the goal and found that he was a natural. Ederson is known for his precise passes and dramatic saves. He is also known as a goalkeeper who stays focused and calm under pressure. Ederson is the backup goalkeeper for the Brazilian national team. He plays primarily in a Kelly green or bright yellow kit for Manchester city.

Goalkeepers often wear padded clothing to protect themselves from collisions with the goal, the ground, and other players. Even so, an injury sustained during practice kept Claudio Bravo off the field for much of 2018.

The Coaches

Current **head coach** Pep Guardiola refuses to do one-on-one **interviews** with reporters before or after games. He prefers to do only large-scale press conferences.

Pep Guardiola is known for his careful attention to detail. He is even particular about the length of the grass on the pitch and prefers that it not grow taller than 0.75 inches (19 millimeters).

Coaches have played an important role in the ups and downs of Manchester City. About 40 coaches have led the team since it was founded. Three of the club's "golden ages" were marked by the leadership of three specific coaches. These are Wilf Wild, Joe Mercer, and current coach Pep Guardiola.

PEP GUARDIOLA Pep Guardiola has been City's head coach since 2016. He is considered one of the best and most innovative coaches in the world. Guardiola has coached at two of Europe's biggest clubs, Barcelona and Bayern Munich. While at Barcelona, he became the youngest coach ever to win the Champions League. Guardiola's strategy involves maintaining possession, adjusting formation based on opponents, and total football, where players move into and out of positions to cover the field.

JOE MERCER Joe Mercer led City to more trophies than any other coach in team history. Mercer was coach at Manchester City from 1965 to 1971. He brought Manchester City out of a losing slump and coached the team back to the first division. City went on to win five trophies with Mercer as coach, including the club's first European title, the European Cup Winners' Cup. Nicknamed "Gentleman Joe," Mercer was known for being soft-spoken and mannerly.

WILF WILD Wilf Wild was Manchester City's head coach from 1932 to 1946. Wild was City's longest-serving coach, but he did not coach the most games because soccer was put on hold during World War II. Wild led Manchester City to its second FA Cup in 1934, the team's first title in 30 years. City also won its first-ever First Division title under his leadership.

Fans Around the World

Manchester City fans are loyal to their club through both golden ages and low points. Fans call their team's ups and downs "typical City" because their beloved Blues have followed the pattern for decades.

Manchester City Supporters Club has 170 branches around the world. The number of City fans has increased by more than 500 percent in recent years. Average attendance for home matches has been around 54,000 since 2015. City has 6.5 million Twitter followers and more than 35 million Facebook followers. The club's official smartphone app provides highlights and live streams. City even has an app for kids.

Fans perform many chants, songs, and dances during games. Manchester City fans' official anthem is "Blue Moon." They also wave scarves, signs, and huge banners at games. Before home matches, fans gather to cheer as the team arrives at Etihad Stadium. A website run by fans keeps City supporters informed about events and game-day activities.

Fan Traditions

#1 A City fan once brought a giant inflatable banana to a game, and now it is a tradition for fans to bring inflatables, especially bananas, to home and away matches.

#2 City fans do the "Poznan," a dance named after a Polish team whose fans introduced the move at a match. Fans turn their backs to the pitch and jump up and down when a goal is scored.

Legends of the Past

Many great players have suited up for Manchester City. A few of them have become icons of the team and the city it represents.

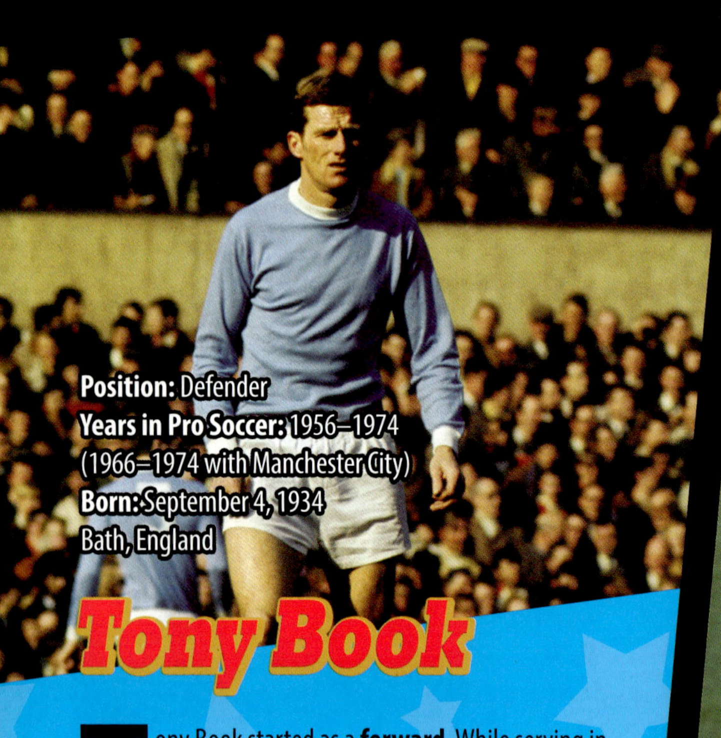

Position: Defender
Years in Pro Soccer: 1956–1974 (1966–1974 with Manchester City)
Born: September 4, 1934 Bath, England

Tony Book

Tony Book started as a **forward**. While serving in the military, he played on an army soccer team and was placed in a defensive position. He remained a **defender** for the rest of his career. Book was made captain of City after his first year on the team. He led the team during one of its golden eras. Book helped City win five trophies, including the European Cup Winners' Cup in 1970. He is considered one of the club's most influential players of all time. Book served as head coach at Manchester City, as well as a temporary coach on four different occasions.

Mike Summerbee

Mike Summerbee spent much of his career with Manchester City. He scored 67 goals in more than 400 appearances for City. Summerbee was a fast, intimidating player who could barrel through defenders to get to the goal. He won six league titles with Manchester City, five in the first division and one in the second division. He was also part of England's national team. After retiring, Summerbee appeared in the soccer-themed World War II film *Victory* starring Pelé, Sylvester Stallone, and Michael Caine. He also owned a men's fashion boutique in Manchester with friend and Manchester United rival George Best.

Position: Forward
Years in Pro Soccer: 1959–1979 (1965–1975 with Manchester City)
Born: December 15, 1942, Preston, England

Bert Trautmann

Bert Trautmann came to England as a German war prisoner during World War II. After he was released, he stayed in England to play soccer. Trautmann had natural goalkeeper instincts. He had a keen sense of where to be, quick reflexes, and a willingness to dive after the ball. Trautmann quickly became one of the best keepers in England. In the 1956 FA Cup final, Trautmann dove for a ball and collided with an opposing player's knee. He was treated on the sideline and finished the game. Doctors later discovered that his neck was broken. Although he was told he would never play again, Trautmann returned the following season.

Position: Goalkeeper
Years in Pro Soccer: 1943–1964 (1949–1964 with Manchester City)
Born: October 22, 1923, Bremen, Germany (Died July 19, 2013)

Colin Bell

Midfielder Colin Bell is considered the best player in Manchester City's history. Nicknamed "the King," Bell scored 152 goals for Manchester City. He was so good that City's assistant coach spread a rumor that Bell could not head the ball and was "hopeless" so that other teams would stop scouting him. Bell played in three cup finals with City and won two of them, along with five more trophies during his career. Bell was also captain of England's national team. He is considered one of the top 50 English players of all time. Bell's career ended when he was only 29 because of a knee injury.

Position: Midfielder
Years in Pro Soccer: 1963–1980 (1966–1979 with Manchester City)
Born: February 26, 1946 Hesleden, England

Stars of Today

Today's Manchester City team is made up of many young, talented players who have proven that they are among the best in the league.

Vincent Kompany

Vincent Kompany started as a midfielder but moved into a **right back** position over time. He became a dominant force in City's defense. Kompany was named Premier League Player of the Season in 2010 and became City's captain at the start of the 2011 season. Kompany is known for scoring on **set pieces** such as corner kicks and free kicks. At the close of the 2017–18 season, he became City's most successful captain ever, with nine trophies and the first 100-point season of the club's history. Kompany is also a member of the Belgian national team and played in five games of the 2018 World Cup.

Position: Defender
Years in Pro Soccer: 2003–Present (Joined City in 2008)
Born: April 10, 1986, Uccle, Belgium

David Silva

David Silva is considered one of Europe's best midfielders. He is nicknamed "Merlin" and "*el Mago*," or "the Magician," by fans and teammates because of his footwork. He has also been referred to as a "conductor" who directs the pace of a game like an orchestra. Silva has eight trophies with Manchester City. He has scored around 70 goals and earned more than 100 assists. Silva is known for his dribbling skills and the ability to maintain possession of the ball, as well as reading the field and making good passing decisions. He has also scored 37 goals in 129 games for Spain's national team.

Position: Midfielder
Years in Pro Soccer: 2004–Present (Joined City in 2010)
Born: January 8, 1986, Arguineguín, Spain

Sergio Agüero

Sergio Agüero was the Premier League's 2014 Golden Boot winner for most goals scored. Agüero has scored more than 200 goals in a little more than 300 games for the club. He scored the game-winning goal in the 2012 Premier League final that won Manchester City the league title. Agüero is a game changer who only needs a moment to create a scoring opportunity for himself or a teammate. Some of his strengths include maintaining control of the ball, key passes, and scoring on headers. Agüero has led Manchester City to nine trophies and is a two-time World Cup participant for Argentina.

Position: Forward
Years in Pro Soccer: 2003–Present (Joined City in 2011)
Born: June 2, 1988, Buenos Aires, Argentina

Kevin De Bruyne

City head coach Pep Guardiola calls Kevin De Bruyne one of the best players he's seen in his life. De Bruyne is a quick thinker and has the ability to read and act on what a game needs. He is also able to make plays and create scoring opportunities for himself and his teammates. De Bruyne's strengths range from ball control, key passes, and scoring from a distance to defensive positioning and long crosses. De Bruyne has scored more than 30 goals and earned nearly 60 assists for Manchester City. He is also part of the Belgian national team and played in the 2014 and 2018 World Cups.

Position: Midfielder
Years in Pro Soccer: 2008–Present (Joined City in 2015)
Born: June 28, 1991, Drongen, Belgium

All-Time Records

100
Most Points in a Season
Manchester City finished the 2017–18 season with a team record of 100 points.

18
Longest Win Streak
Manchester City won 18 games in a row in 2017, setting a team record.

680
Most Games Played
Midfielder Alan Oakes played a Manchester City record 680 games from 1959 to 1976.

84,569

Record Attendance

City's record attendance for a single game was during the 1933–34 season, when 84,569 people attended a match against Stoke City at Maine Road stadium.

49

Oldest Player

Manchester City legend Billy Meredith was 49 when he played his last game in blue, making him the oldest player ever to take the field for the team.

Timeline

Throughout the team's history, Manchester City has had many memorable events that have become defining moments for the team and its fans.

1880
Anna Connell leads the formation of a men's sports club that will eventually become Manchester City.

1889
City wins the Division Two title and becomes the first team to be automatically promoted to the First Division.

1880 | 1890 | 1900 | 1920 | 1930 | 1940 | 1950

In 1894, the team officially becomes Manchester City Football Club.

1937
The Blues win the Division One championship for the first time.

1904
Manchester City wins its first Football Association Cup.

1970
The Blues win the League Cup and their first European title, the European Cup Winners' Cup.

2003
The club moves into the City of Manchester Stadium, later known as Etihad Stadium.

The Future
Currently number one in the Premier League, Manchester City is enjoying its greatest golden age yet. City's roster is filled with seasoned players and young talent. Pep Guardiola and his dynamic Blues have the potential to match their record-breaking 2017–18 season.

1960 | 1970 | 1980 | 1990 | 2000 | 2010 | 2020

In 1992, the Premier League is established with Manchester City as a founding member.

2008
The Abu Dhabi United Group purchases Manchester City, transforming it into one of the world's most valuable sports clubs.

2018
Pep Guardiola leads the Blues to one of the most successful seasons in Premier League history, finishing 19 points ahead of the second-place team.

Write a Biography

Life Story

A person's life story can be the subject of a book. This kind of book is called a biography. Biographies often describe the lives of people who have achieved great success. These people may be alive today, or they may have lived many years ago. Reading a biography can help you learn more about a great person.

Get the Facts

Use research in the library and on the internet to find out more about your favorite soccer player. Learn as much about him or her as you can. What position does he or she play? What are his or her statistics in important categories? Has he or she set any records? Also, be sure to write down key events in the person's life. What was his or her childhood like? What has he or she accomplished off the field? Is there anything else that makes this person special or unusual?

Use the Concept Web

A concept web is a useful research tool. Read the questions in the concept web on the following page. Answer the questions in your notebook. Your answers will help you write a biography.

Concept Web

Adulthood
- Where does this individual currently reside?
- Does he or she have a family?

Your Opinion
- What did you learn from the books you read in your research?
- Would you suggest these books to others?
- Was anything missing from these books?

Childhood
- Where and when was this person born?
- Describe his or her parents, siblings, and friends.
- Did this person grow up in unusual circumstances?

Accomplishments off the Field
- What is this person's life's work?
- Has he or she received awards or recognition for accomplishments?
- How have this person's accomplishments served others?

Help and Obstacles
- Did this individual have a positive attitude?
- Did he or she receive help from others?
- Did this person have a mentor?
- Did this person face any hardships?
- If so, how were the hardships overcome?

Accomplishments on the Field
- What records does this person hold?
- What key games and plays have defined his or her career?
- What are this person's stats in categories important to his or her position?

Work and Preparation
- What was this person's education?
- What was his or her work experience?
- How does this person work?
- What is the process he or she uses?

Trivia Time

Take this quiz to test your knowledge of Manchester City. The answers are printed upside down under each question.

1 Which team is Manchester City's biggest rival?

A. Manchester United

2 Who is considered the founder of Manchester City?

A. Anna Connell

3 How many times has Manchester City won the Premier League title since 2011?

A. Three

4 What was the original name of Etihad Stadium?

A. City of Manchester Stadium

5 Which Manchester City coach has won the most trophies?

A. Joe Mercer

6 What unique objects do City fans often bring to home and away matches?

A. Inflatables, including inflatable bananas

7 What soccer-themed World War II film featured Manchester City legend Mike Summerbee?

A. *Victory*

8 Thanks to his fancy footwork, David Silva has been given which nicknames by fans?

A. "Merlin" and "*el Mago*," or "the Magician"

9 How many points did Manchester City have at the end of the 2017–2018 season?

A. 100

Key Words

clubs: athletic teams or organizations

Commonwealth Games: an international multi-sport competition played by the Commonwealth Nations, including Great Britain, Australia, and Canada

defender: also called a "back," a player who plays in front of the goal and stops the other team from scoring

forward: a player on a soccer team who normally plays closest to the opponent's goal and tries to score goals

goalkeepers: also called "goalies," players responsible for keeping the ball from going into the goal and the only players who are allowed to pick up the ball

kit: the standard attire and equipment worn by soccer players, including a jersey, shorts, socks, and shin guards

midfielder: a soccer player who plays between the forwards and defenders and can take either a defensive or offensive role

pitch: an area that is used for playing sports

relegated: moved to a lower rank or division

right back: a defensive field player who plays to the goalkeeper's right

set pieces: situations in which the ball is returned to play after a penalty or foul; some examples include corner kicks and free kicks

Index

Log on to www.av2books.com

AV² by Weigl brings you media enhanced books that support active learning. Go to www.av2books.com, and enter the special code found on page 2 of this book. You will gain access to enriched and enhanced content that supplements and complements this book. Content includes video, audio, weblinks, quizzes, a slide show, and activities.

AV² Online Navigation

Book Pages
AV² pages directly correspond to pages in the book.

Audio
Listen to sections of the book read aloud.

Video
Watch informative video clips.

Embedded Weblinks
Gain additional information for research.

Key Words
Study vocabulary, and complete a matching word activity.

Try This!
Complete activities and hands-on experiments.

Quizzes
Test your knowledge.

Slide Show
View images and captions, and prepare a presentation.

AV² was built to bridge the gap between print and digital. We encourage you to tell us what you like and what you want to see in the future.

Sign up to be an AV² Ambassador at www.av2books.com/ambassador.

Due to the dynamic nature of the Internet, some of the URLs and activities provided as part of AV² by Weigl may have changed or ceased to exist. AV² by Weigl accepts no responsibility for any such changes. All media enhanced books are regularly monitored to update addresses and sites in a timely manner. Contact AV² by Weigl at 1-866-649-3445 or av2books@weigl.com with any questions, comments, or feedback.